NOON
NOUR KAMEL

Published by Akashic Books
©2019 Nour Kamel

ISBN: 978-1-61775-744-0

Akashic Books
Brooklyn, New York, USA
Ballydehob, Co. Cork, Ireland
Twitter: @AkashicBooks
Facebook: AkashicBooks
E-mail: info@akashicbooks.com
Website: www.akashicbooks.com

African Poetry Book Fund
Prairie Schooner
University of Nebraska
110 Andrews Hall
Lincoln, Nebraska 68588

TABLE OF CONTENTS

The brilliance of Nour Kamel in this chapbook, *Noon*, lies in the way the poet is constantly disrupting, reengaging, challenging, and pushing the boundaries of what we think we know about self and other. You may not believe me.

Language is a gossip, a tatterdemalion, an unreliable witness of the world and its affairs. Still, there is a delicate balance between language and reality, between language and order and the very power of language to reassure. In this beautifully destabilizing book, the poet questions language's ability to create a coherence of place, of country, of self, and of identity. There is play, for sure, and punning, but there is also an impression of an unrestrained hysteria; the sense of desperation one feels when one calls out for understanding and is always misread. Even the act of speaking creates more obfuscation than clarity. Nevertheless, in this poet's hands, by a curious act of alchemy, this confrontational and juxtapositional relationship of language to itself results in a new syntax, a new rhetoric—one that can facilitate a certain transformation and thus allow a new possibility to cohere.

In the poem "Bata Soda," for instance, the personal, the "i," is not capitalized and the "You," both personal and communal, is. From the very beginning, the poet builds a narrative thrust of a compounded, multi-valanced identity:

> i carry You like the moon carries the months.

These poems nod to narrative, though, while they contain that gesture, they immediately undermine it by way of strange juxtapositions and impossible constructs. Again, in the poem Bata Soda, we have lines like:

> a ram and the sun play hot potato with my liver.

Painting an image that represents what can only be an impossibility. And yet, the unadorned manner of this construct allows the reader to accept what is incongruous with graceful ease. As a result, singular meaning is defeated, and perhaps even actual meaning too, leaving instead only a careful balance of simultaneity, where one thing stands next to the other, not necessarily in harmony or in agreement, but standing together nonetheless.

Of course, the image of the ram and the sun gestures to the ancient Egyptian heliographic; at once history and loss—the loss of language and identity to time—the lack of direct meaning in the image forces a symbolic and alchemical relationship, challenging modern linguistic constructs of narrative that are reductive and transactional in nature. However, the trick of images like this is that they challenge our belief or acceptance of essential identities, without ever seeming to do so.

In deft lines, the poet argues for, against, and with singular identities, singular stories, forcing an uncomfortable but oddly noncontradictory sense of difference and multiplicity to flourish. And yet, for all of this, the address of most of the poems here is to the beloved, and to all who love. In this way, love becomes the vehicle, love becomes the underlying linguistic structure—love as eros, the most creative power in the universe; but also love as that which often limits, unintentionally or intentionally, all our possibility.

In the opening sequence of the poem "Isis in Mohandessin for my Birth," the poet, in addition to punning on Isis—state, goddess, and archetype, starts from the divine, with reference to wings, moves to the quotidian, with the washing on the clothesline, then to the entire geographical area of Egypt and the Mediterranean, including bordering states like ancient Greece. The poet then speaks of the loss of knowledge, and sense of self, with the destruction of the Colossus of Crete and the burning of the library at Alexandria—at one time the pinnacle of knowledge for the world—and arrives at their birth, the poet's birth, in time in the name. Brilliant, bold, and daring political and personal control of history, self, identity, and the body:

Some high feathered wisdom was lost and balanced on a clothesline

along the same sea Athena was being worshiped, though further inland
congested, without the fabulousness of lost Colossus and a burning library,
I was born at noon.

In poems like "Hypothetical body equation (with cats)," the poet creates a
powerful set of lines juxtaposed to amalgamate into meaning, rather than argue
for an existing one. There is nothing essential here, nothing we can trust to fully
hold us up, nothing that is considered more important than anything else; the
entire journey here is an enactment of the process of negotiating identity—how
we come to body and to self if we allow ourselves not to buy into patterns and
bodies already imagined for us—simultaneously creating rupture and repair, and
allowing the conversations about gender, sexuality, body, adornment, and choice
to be robust, fluid, and accessible.

What does this mean? It means that in this chapbook of highly original
and syntactically complex forms, it would be easy to consider these poems
and the drive here as experimental, as displacements from the norm intended
to bring a certain attention to what we would normally see as "poetry," closer
to something we think of as language poetry. But that would be a mistake. It
would also be a mistake to read these poems as strict narrative arguments and
explorations. What is here is more complex than that in its process, narrative,
enactment, and displacement and reenactment of sexuality, identity, place, history, culture, feminism, and more.

The urge here is a sincere and urgent wrestling with and against the fact
that one language, or linguistic mode, cannot hold the simultaneity of being
"African," "female," "woman," etc., and so disrupts singularity.

The last line of that poem, "Hypothetical body equation (with cats)," is so mas-
terful, because it both ends that dueling process and simultaneously continues it.

So I named my body Come, and I'll let it call what it needs.

Enjoy the talent of Nour Kamel.

BATA SODA

if there's an equivalent for black sheep in arabic i don't know it
whoever You are i carry You like the moon carries the months
i don't want to let You down and You wouldn't imagine me
lost between calendars and a goofy tide

a ram and the sun play hot potato with my liver, the sun
makes to catch it, the galaxy quivers and my liver dries up
making it to her arms never. they sell it to a food truck
You eat me drenched in tahina on soft french bread

i wrote this poem seven times in stops, 3 times fast 4 times slow
traced with red skin your calligraphy, your cursive bones
too big to curse You with but the meaning of a kid
whose word is only love really.

this is the part where i can still be You,
but i couldn't wrap my head around a peach, my jaw
chews the pit clicking kho kho khokh and you're veiled
rolling eyes at a tongue that calls anything but mama

there is only one word in your mouth, You feign others to get by
we aren't so different then, there is an off-yellow-sickly prickly pear
You swallow every summer seed to flesh ratio phenomenal pebbles
find the hollows of your teeth hopeful for what might blossom

maybe you'd think i was silly and want to know too much
when there's god so how can we be lost inside our own skin
the ram thinks me redeemable she etches into my side
a sun tattoo, rings of words i can't read on my own

as i watch mute

there's an equivalent for black sheep in arabic

and i'm sure i don't know it

ISIS IN MOHANDESSIN FOR MY BIRTH

Some high feathered wisdom was lost and balanced on a clothesline
along the same sea Athena was being worshipped, though further inland
congested, without the fabulousness of lost colossus and a burning library,
I was born at noon

Doctors inside my mother, doctors above her bellyup and full of me
I came into the word at an angle sword in sheath shoulder first poised
to raise my dagger in battle I would wage from that day til this day
and onwards and onwards and onwards little horsie

But the doctors shook my grip loose, pushed the breadth of me back
into womb, into abandon, into her, my sword lost, I came with nothing
between my legs proclaimed girl with two holes two golden hoops bled
in each ear gender stigmata

Jesus, wept and weeping, would not be waiting like the lost white owl
we shared a crowning glory tho of golden halo wire hovering above head
an afro for always untamable, a warning, ruffled and bigger than
my edible body

Flew through skies getting too filled forever with doomsday shade. Isis,
why were you calling after me: was I stolen from the underworld by mama's will,
or did you last minute bless kiss my parts together with purposeful eyes halfseeing
a blurred world for what it is

Whatever prophecy you gave, mama said it was an omen with worrycast eyes
of things to fight unarmed vulnerable because they told me I was, all mixed up
too pale to be born me in the not-moon, who couldn't help wage the kind of war
my legs meant me for

Women's work women worry women gods! she didn't see if it was good or bad, double-glazed reflective glass, saw a lost portent of her feathered self something brief something that would kill with just a sheath, in silence looming, doubled, eat you head, first, whole.

HYPOTHETICAL BODY EQUATION (WITH CATS)

So they make me fall in love with what I could never love whole. What mascara do you use? You have beautiful eyelashes masha2allah. Compliments praising gods work and not you. I want to be the extremes of myself and dress in drag. King. Queen. A boat. where. is the line. though where can I be the utmost of myself if not on public transportation. To and fro to and fro, the ashes had me at don't mind the gap. I try not to burn up too soon and fall. Feel parts of me have, scooping imaginary limbs I had briefly before forgetting forever.

So I went and made you, because everything where I was was too much. I gathered the drek, discarded cat bones, everything that had a hole in it that couldn't be mended. Loose drippings from the pan. I turned everything unwanted my chest could expand to breathe in into you. I named you Home and called you Beaut. Now the drek has turned the alive of green, the cats know where their bones are buried, and patchwork isn't something the poor do mama to hide their bodies. I'd let you light the world when it got darkest but sometimes you say the stupidest shit and you won't let me bring anymore cats Home.

So I named my body Come, and I'll let it call what it needs.

NO ONE LOVES ANYONE AND WE ALL HAVE INTIMATE DEEP RELATIONSHIPS

who likes getting their hair wet
any black child will tell you it's hell
when it's ready for a comb in a heavy hand

young, wetness was too much, suffocating
I swam head above water crocodileeyes on
my mother's hands, are mine, but her hair isn't

she combed out my hair as if she could the kinks,
wrap her hand around its expanding body
wearing me a guest of its dominion

when my hair is wet is when the ridges align
see the beauty in the order of honeycomb
fragile beauty in the chaos buzz of bees

I am amazed by the depths of what water can do
with kinky mermaid hair grown long for you, but now
I will make a home between saudi and the red sea

I unpack my heart first before taking off my shoes
it gets confused when I change elevation
now, I am neptune's flippers

iridescent to the eye that catches me
my hair billows, fish mistake it for a coral home
in the depths I won't know what depressed is

a state of being, or being, the depths won't expect
that I have known love and other people's body
hair between closed closed ridges and folds

the depths and I will look at each other
and then I'll make us some tea
earl grey with date molasses

Everyone loves everyone and we all don't have to know each other

WOMAN LOOKING FOR THE DISAPPEARED DISAPPEARS ON WAY TO CONFERENCE ON DISAPPEARANCES

look, people just go missing here
what could be more female than that
to go missing with no one to claim you
were ever there

to speak a woman's existence
demands her existence
does she exist if

there is no blood
no virginity tests
no orbital wounds
ashed over

what can be more violent than never knowing
in which way the bodies were taken
does she exist if all that's left

are her shoes
some heartache
the memory that

I've never walked a street alone
forgetting who I am but goddamn
I'll fake my safety til they believe it too

until trust is not just family
life is lived above ground
love can be in color

we are the missing, forced
disappearances are causality if you're cruel
are oxymoron if you still have a sense of humor

what is the function of femininity except survive in danger

my female body is for their violence on the daily
who has our bravery
plucked out of soft palms

if we rain it down on them
do we become the bloody invisible
drenched in it to live

maybe   lets live

before they bring the dying for us
with a silencing and our soldered off parts
they keep in trophy closets

LINEAGE

My baba says everyone in his family is egyptian with a twinkle in his green eyes
(he sees the doubt in mine), except for his grandfather the greeneyed turk, but
everyone else was egyptian all the way back, truly.

My mother, like a true egyptian, knows but doesn't care where her people came
from. Somewhere she calls upper egypt and my sister collects ashes of informa-
tion and tells me we are maternally iranian and nubian, which explains both our
hair respectively.

My pops says the romeros were spanish and not mexican, they had blonde hair
and blue eyes (according to him), that grandma (his) was an aztec and that's
why he's so dark and ugly (he isn't) and she lived to a hundred.

I always thought we were all an amalgam of each other because how could I be
three when most were two? it didn't make sense to tell people I was anything
but american, knew jingles from the 50s and said sangitch instead of sandwich.
strangers know we are sisters but she looks like her dad and I look like our
mom and there must have been some osmosis of emotions going on something
not lost in the space between a womb shared. there are parts inside my mother that are my sister that are my pops and here I am. our brother, somewhere.
I knew this, as a kid and forgot it, somewhere, when another kid said you
shouldn't call each other sister.

RECURRING HAUNT

the fruit bowl goes flying across rooms
shattered wood breaks off your father
he waits until the ghost stops heaving

kunafa like golden hair, scattered
food her hands made to break our fast
your mother finds a broom in her stomach

the ghost is deaf
to your pleadings
you teach yourself patience and sign language

a water jug was destined for your head
the floor made enough of an ashtray
ectoplasm spat in corners leaving stains

neighbors know their business
is not to get involved with yours
hauntings are exorcised behind closed doors

the ghost stinks
of weed and smoke
you place comfort at the source, and hope

the quiet outweighs the violent
it only comes out about twice a year
and he used to be such a good boy

the one that would bring broken birds home

blatantly cheat at games with such glory
wide eyes made you fall in love like a mother

the ghost lets you
bless the house, burn incense
bring a sheikh to whisper words

we shake on it and agree to go on
living somewhat gaslit, terrified
pretending we're all alright

because have you ever heard a deaf ghostboy laugh?

it's like god, singing

LADY FINGERS

arrested by the smell of
I forget the words
as I bite into its bitterness
know it as habahan
before cardamom ever reaches

know rosemary and parsley and thyme both ways w irfa w kuzbara w filfil

don't know the word for dill
never forget its sharp fresh taste
in mama's ma7shi

is the tongue inherited béchamel licked off fingers from pots it was just like mama

know it pick it eat it dill
I have no idea what it is
on my mother's tongue

image of her making the same supplicant movements of joyous food grace before

couldn't say khokh
but bruised as easy
as the sweet flesh
sank into poolside
summer peaches

her mother putting saneya into fire gas oven turned electric who knows where
you'll be

come morning, coffee
is not coffee made
on flame-filled stovetops
americano coffee
only mustered the day

cooking or if you'll be looking upon another you and feed this feeling of endlessness

ours set the course
of arabian nights
tells tales told well
in the dusk

with whose word for what taste if genetic string binds they'll love and call it
  bamya too

THINK ABOUT ALL THE PEOPLE WHO LOOK AT YOU IN A DAY

people watching becomes people staring

a national pastime
who can be the most cruel
about another person's body.

I forget what I look like.
dress for comfort and
dress to comfort

think about if I'll have to walk in the street

and if so which one
and if so what time

will I have to take the metro
and if so what time

and will the women's carriage be empty
and will the women's carriage be full

will women stare at me eyes wide in humorous terror
mouths moving quiet whispers to make each other as small

as other eyes have made them feel

when I want to smile, tell you

you have beautiful eyelashes masha2allah
stretchmarks on your arms match mine
you look like my mother
like women I love

do you get stared at in the street
for wearing that too

and if so what time

HOME

the smell of wet dust that means rain
rain that only smells that way here
car rides with boys who have cars
and girls who are given cars by male relatives

who ask you if it's okay to smoke in front
on you windows rolled down driving
too fast the wind and smoke dont have time
to relate get trapped travelled disappear into each other

like you wish you could
her certainty and uncertainties
at least they would not be your own.
you would be empty and safe and home inside her.

that nervous tic motion of the head
follows every boy you try to know
every boy who tries to embed himself in your heart,
very boyish, every body who demands you make a feddan

for his feelings and empty yourself out no,
does not even know you are full acres of your own.
doesnt know the bitten lip and silence
that metal is in your throat keeping

the tears down because you learnt too early emotions were
      for girls
and boys
      were better for lack, modelled yourself on a failing sex

then learned to, pleaded with the other
to have you back, wounded and broken
and not sure how to find home inside yourself
or others

only making room for others
so you claw your way into their bodies
roost and make a home that will not hurt
you only in the end, in the end, only then

when you pull back the hand
nails entrenched in your heart of hearts
and they never forgive you
for not being you.

THANKSGIVING BREAK

after Ayoola and Shakespeare

Do you remember that time I came all
the way from Mississippi to San Fran
cisco to see you and surprised you at
your front door half your braids unbraided. You
screamed I thought you were dying you told me
I was the worst. You couldn't stop touching
me. Conditioned combed washed your hair I read
a comic and was sad at the transi
ent nature of existence. We went thrift
ing on Mission and ate a Farolit
o burrito. Going to the wrong the
atre early, we talked about death while
I thought about ice cream waiting for a
screening I didn't want to see. We tried

not to laugh at the drunk Super Duper
Burger boy, watching people watch people.
I waited exploring as you threaded
your hair for painful hours. Coit, I climbed,
was closed, until spring, but up top, I heard,
the barks, below. Hills going, late, the wrong
direction back to you, "I would climb it,
scale this city on bad hips and weak knees."
Thinking in the breeze, horribly human
imagining—heroics. We went to
Dr. Teeth and you provided an in
troduction to people you half-not liked:
Julian the German who looked at me
and remembered my name, a Grecian face

that belonged pouting in a museum
Peter who didn't look like much Owen
who could have been anyone Evan face
scrunched-bitter mouth confused then gaping a
round the vowels too copious and close
for him in my name, who wore a hat in
doors atop, beneath: an unremarka
bly handsome face and a hole in an ear
where redness spread. Lumbering towards Lombard
I look for a knoll to sit and roll down.
We held hands on the bridge and people smiled
at us lesbian lovers. You said that
there would be fog but sun shone and we roamed
through a park with bison and a heron

that hunted a mouse with precision and
patience. You exulted, I whimpered. The
entire city smelt of pine? You did
n't know. What I imagine verbena
must smell like from its syllables. The cit
rus smell of lemon lime verbena? Pine.
What was it that California smelled like
home thin air grassy minty lemons, leaves.
To Castro, with pride, then the paradox
of Valencia vs. Mission, streets
apart. Showing me the bars you frequent
without me Blondies Radio Haban
a Social Club. On thanksgiving we climbed
both peaks of Twin Peaks at my behest, though

one would have been enough. And looked into
all the pretty rich houses with people
possibly in them but where no one seemed
to live. I noted all the people out
that day and wondered why they were alone
why like us foreign nomads they were not
in a home partaking. Thought, this time last
year, I had made a friend enough of you
to ask you to eat with me and others,
heed a holiday I knew little of,
give thanks for the existence of turkey,
greens, collard, gravy, wine, potato, sweet.
We sat in Carl's Jr. sweet potato
fries. I wondered if you remembered that.

THE ARAB WOMAN OF THE FUTURE

is date molasses and tehina
fed to mouths made bellyful
has never known
all the kinds of hunger
a body and soul can pang for

measures herself against
what was once called an oriental
rug and thinks
the stitching simple
color sanitized and muted

has never heard the saying
il mekhalifa bint masnooda
bil kheit, wil mekhalifa walad
masnooda bil heit
it is indecipherable across time

knows where her vagina is
has no idea that her foremothers
held down her foremothers
turned all the pleasure of her body
a scar, a budded wound

reads in history books
about something called a hymen
that was prized by the ancients
dictated the worth of her sex
by lecherous, respectable men

feels blood flow freely
between her legs, introduces her mother
to her menstrual cup
instead of crying, she responds
"how environmentally friendly"

grows the body of her hair
or sets it all aflame to nothing
covers herself to eyes
or nothing
laid bare on a prayer rug

marries no one and her family
celebrates her with a zaffa
daily hennaed bodies dancing
a bridal cloth isn't
but an unburnished web of white

goes to her father
tells him her secret desires
he smiles, lies, says
the landscape of the world
has always been hers

does not need protecting
is not ravished by eyes
listens to night sounds of her city
not words that would bend her
into nonexistence

takes a lover, takes
a thousand and one
no cares between thighs
all draped in galabeyas
stitched unshut and blooming

gives birth to her children
they are of her body hers
she needs no one
to insist their existence
she voices her sound

everyone listens
she has said
something

knows thread holds
older than walls
reused, restitched, repaired
ends at those who cut it
but never ends

chooses each patterned color
in the tapestry of her lifetime
without second

(
listen

she doesn't know

any of this

lets not break it

what

are the chances

history continues

repeats
)

AIRPORTS

I saw a little girl
with her toy piggy
in Paris

on our way to Cairo
where I swore
we were both London-bound

perhaps
almost
two years ago

the mother with her mother
and the little girl
with her piggy.

the curls
the forehead
gold hoop earrings

her face in profile
beside her mother's
the same in miniature

a shade between
light mother
dark father

how amazing

whatever
coincidence is

they don't remember me
that they wouldn't
that I would

be distraught and doubt
precocious
hennaed hands.

RAET MEETS ME AT BEHOOS

if I cry on a Cairo street alone tear my face apart like this city does kindness
someone will demand I immediately stop
pull up the consolation of a chair from nowhere in the middle of the street w
    kobayit shay[1]
someone will say malik ya binti[2] and I will be the universal daughter that Ra
    couldn't live without
someone shaped like mama will shove a shush and something sweetened
into my supplicant mouth that has forgotten every name of god
except my own

someone I love a woman tells me I've lost weight   wait like
Where did I go What has hollowed me out and Have I done this to myself
have I pulled the abaya[3] tight to my body revealed the rolls of scripture I keep
only for myself, hastily hidden them for safety so well I've forgotten how to pray
to my body

the sun god had only daughters, or wives, an either/or type mythology blurred
that Ra herself could get away with being more than one grow herself fat for loving
soon you won't feel the ribs poke through their shadow rippling underneath
    your skin
every breath breakable

I dream about crushing the men who would eat me between my pillowy thighs
grow my hair thick on air like I taught it it doesn't need shit to live but my hands
Raet gives herself both names to survive in time, in fracture, she knew a part
must be lost, a part attached to our names, that they'll acknowledged all the work
our body endures

---

1   made loose leaf and sugar heaped
2   said half-exasperated
3   not black, no, never

once I started believing it I could count through my limbs everyone who branded
    me beautiful
told me I was in their moment something rare they'd seen everyday the sunrise
confused for sunset at just the right moment they caught the clarity of me knew
I moved through the world like I moved it
I am sun, god

JONAH AND THE WHALE

Younes, in a careem,
I half understood a man who had refound god, asked me if I knew the story of
sayedna younes. I said no and he explained younes turned his back on god and
then there was a safina and they needed to get rid of the bodies on it and they
threw them off

as younes threw himself off a whale sent by god came up and swallowed him
and as they say jonah lived in the belly of the whale and Jonah! yes jonah, jonah
and the whale. A story I didn't know either but there was a hoot, and jonah
found himself in it for some time there some somewhere heard knew the en-
glish words bas younes. Mein younes? Younes w•el hoot.

Hoot hoot hoot.

I said 40 days inside
40 being a biblical number I had found, he admitted he didn't know it was
maybe between 3 and 40 but how long does one last in a whale anyway we
arrived and talked about other same things like god and he told me the moral
but I forgot it. Something about

turning our backs about why we are always rushing why we never like the
beginning of the week and crave the end because the end the finishing gets us
closer to rabena cause we want to be with her, yes her, if I had said her he would
have crashed us into the nile perhaps with no big fish to save our undivine
behinds but him isn't right either and what a language we have

with genders and endings you have to know and remember even for the creator
of everything and creator you know is gender neutral.

UNSOLVABLE BODY EQUATION

If a train leaves from cairo where does it go. rhodes would have made it cairo to capetown but we all know what happened to him. Nothing. the niqabi on the train wears gloves with a hole in one finger, the index, and your eyes are peeping through that slit, waiting for her to point you in the direction of history. If a train leaves from belen, new mexico it will never go anywhere again. pops tells you about every girl who called him ugly in between every euphemism he has for gay men, dated circa 1942. If a train leaves home with all your parents on it they stare as if they are all knowing. know the things you think and lie about and will never fully feel. If a train is coming and your body is on the tracks what does that body even look like anymore when everyone is looking at it. no one wants to tell you the train is coming.

ACKNOWLEDGMENTS

My family is my life, without them none of this would have happened. I want to thank the friends who love, support, and encourage me ceaselessly. In particular, Ayoola Solarin—thank you for reading everything I threw at you and helping me put this collection together when I doubted I could. I'd also like to thank and acknowledge all the phenomenal venues and publications that provided a platform for me to develop and publish some of the poems in this collection. These include:

Asameena—"The Arab Woman of the Future"
Anomaly, Egyptian Writers Folio—"Bata Soda"
Winter Tangerine Summer Poetry Workshops, 2017
The Brunel International African Poetry Prize